❦ History *of* Britain ❦

Tudor Explorers

Brian Williams

Illustrated by Mark Bergin

HAMLYN

HISTORY OF BRITAIN –TUDOR EXPLORERS
was produced for Hamlyn Children's Books
by Lionheart Books, London
Editor: Lionel Bender
Designer: Ben White
Editorial Assistant: Madeleine Samuel, Jo Hanks
Picture Researcher: Jennie Karrach
Media Conversion and Typesetting:
  Peter MacDonald
Educational Consultant: Jane Shuter
Editorial Advisors: Andrew Farrow, Paul Shuter
Production Controller: Catherine Bald
Editorial Director: David Riley

First published in Great Britain in 1995
by Hamlyn Children's Books,
an imprint of Reed International Books,
Michelin House, 81 Fulham Road, London SW3 6RB,
and Auckland, Melbourne, Singapore and Toronto.
ISBN 0 600 58782 7 Hb   ISBN 0 600 58783 5 Pb
British Library Cataloguing-in-Publication Data.
A catalogue record for this book is available
from the British Library.
Printed in China

Acknowledgements
All illustrations by Mark Bergin except maps, by
Hayward Art Group.
Picture credits
BAL = The Bridgeman Art Library, NPG = By courtesy of
the National Portrait Gallery, London, MC = The Mansell
Collection.
l = left, r = right, t = top, b = bottom, c = centre.
Pages: 4t: Anthony Blake Photo Library. 5t: Biblioteca
Estense ed Universitaria di Modena, Italy/Foto Roncaglia.
5b: BAL/City of Bristol Museum & Art Gallery. 6tr: NPG.
6cl: Michael Holford. 7: MC. 8b: BAL/National Maritime
Museum, London. 9: By Courtesy of the Master and
Fellows of Magdalene College, Cambridge. 10: Plymouth
City Museums & Art Gallery Collection. 11t: Hispanic·
Society of America. 11b: Werner Forman Archive. 12l:
Bodleian Library, Oxford. 13t, 13c: BAL/By Courtesy of
the Trustees of the British Museum, London. 13b: With the
Permission of the Marquess of Salisbury, Hatfield House.
14bl: Fotomas Index. 14tr: NPG. 15t: Fotomas Index.
15c: e.t. archive. 16bl: Fotomas Index. 16cr: BAL/New
York Public Library. 17tl: Fotomas Index. 17cr: By
Courtesy of the Master and Fellows of Magdalene College,
Cambridge. 18tl, 18tr: BAL/By Courtesy of the Trustees
of the British Museum, London. 18br: NPG. 19t: BAL/By
Courtesy of the Trustees of the British Museum, London.
19b: MC. 20t: NPG. 20b: Pierpont Morgan Library/Art
Resource/MA 3900. f.97. 21t: Drake Print – Hulton
Deutsch. 21b: MC. 22tr: Historical Society of
Pennsylvania. 22bl: BAL/By Courtesy of the Trustees of
the British Museum, London.
Cover: Artwork by Mark Bergin. Icons by Michael Shoebridge.
Photos: (Frobisher's second voyage & Virginia Colony): BAL/
By Courtesy of the Trustees of the British Museum, London.
(Portrait of Drake): NPG. (English raid): Hulton Deutsch.

PLACES TO VISIT

Here are some museums and sites connected with Tudor
Explorers you can visit, with treasures, statues of famous
seamen, ships and paintings of the time to see.

Berkeley Castle, Gloucestershire. Oak chest from Drake's
cabin on board the *Golden Hind* on its round-the-world
voyage.

Bristol, Avon. Seaport city, with historic trade links with
America. Museum with items from America. A monument
on Brandon Hill commemorates John Cabot.

Buckland Abbey, Devon. Home of Grenville and Drake, now
a museum; banners flown on board the *Golden Hind*.

Burghley House, Huntingdon. Great Tudor mansion, home of
the Cecil family from 1587.

Hampton Court, Surrey. Royal palace, with a great hall built
for King Henry VIII.

Hatfield House, Hertfordshire. House owned by the Cecils,
on the site of a royal palace where Elizabeth lived before
she was queen. Has examples of Raleigh's writings.

National Maritime Museum, Greenwich, London. Pictures,
maps, models and items from ships of the time. Exhibits
include Drake's Dial, his world map and medal.

National Portrait Gallery, London. Paintings of English
leaders and sea captains of the time, including Raleigh.

Plymouth, Devon. Port from which many voyages began.
Museum exhibits include a cup given to Drake by Queen
Elizabeth I.

Portsmouth, Hampshire. Tudor warship *Mary Rose*, restored
and displayed with items found on board to show what life
at sea was like in the mid-1500s.

Tavistock, Devon. Drake's birthplace, and a statue in his
honour.

INTRODUCTION

At the end of the 1400s the Portuguese and Spanish began exploring oceans and lands previously unknown to Europeans. Their ships sailed round Africa to India, and across the Atlantic Ocean to America. English, French and Dutch sailors soon followed, and so began a century of exploration. Throughout the 1500s Europeans explored the new, wider world that was opening up before them. Merchants sought new trade routes. Sailors mapped new seas. Soldiers fought and conquered for gold and silver. Colonists went in search of new lands to settle. The people of Tudor England, ruled by monarchs from Henry VII to Elizabeth I, played a growing part in this adventure.

CONTENTS

A WIDER WORLD

The voyages of Columbus to America (1492) and Magellan round the world (1519-21) proved that the world was larger than Europeans thought. Traders were eager to explore the new lands, hoping to find riches greater even than those of Asia.

In 1522, one ship with 18 seamen left on board returned to Spain. Five ships had set out. The men's leader, Ferdinand Magellan, was dead. They had become the first people to sail round the world.

Europeans, and the Catholic Church, had already divided the 'New World' as if they owned it. By 1540 Spain had seized Mexico and much of South America. Portugal controlled the trade routes by sea round Africa to India, China and Japan. English merchants had to look elsewhere for overseas trade. They hoped to profit from John Cabot's voyages to America.

△ **Spices from Asia, such as pepper and ginger**, were used in Europe to make dried or salted meat and fish more tasty. To bring them overland to Europe took two years. Spices fetched a high price so were worth a risky voyage.

▷ **Some of the great voyages of exploration from western Europe.**
● The Portuguese sailed around Africa. By this route, Vasco da Gama reached India in 1498.
● Columbus and Cabot sailed west across the Atlantic Ocean to 'discover' America.
● Magellan's sailors circled the world.
● The Spaniards Cortés and Pizarro explored parts of Central and South America.
● Jacques Cartier of France landed in Canada.

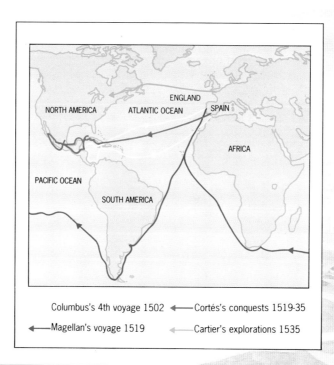

ENGLAND

NORTH AMERICA   ATLANTIC OCEAN   SPAIN

AFRICA

PACIFIC OCEAN

SOUTH AMERICA

Columbus's 4th voyage 1502 ← ── Cortés's conquests 1519-35

← ──Magellan's voyage 1519   Cartier's explorations 1535

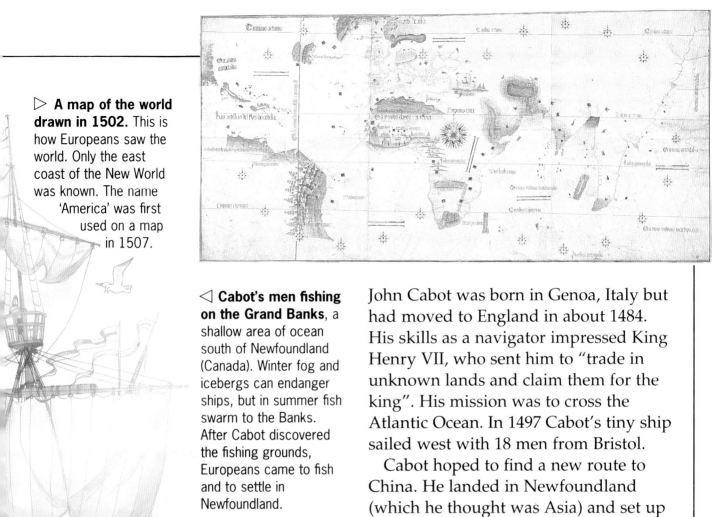

▷ **A map of the world drawn in 1502.** This is how Europeans saw the world. Only the east coast of the New World was known. The name 'America' was first used on a map in 1507.

◁ **Cabot's men fishing on the Grand Banks**, a shallow area of ocean south of Newfoundland (Canada). Winter fog and icebergs can endanger ships, but in summer fish swarm to the Banks. After Cabot discovered the fishing grounds, Europeans came to fish and to settle in Newfoundland.

John Cabot was born in Genoa, Italy but had moved to England in about 1484. His skills as a navigator impressed King Henry VII, who sent him to "trade in unknown lands and claim them for the king". His mission was to cross the Atlantic Ocean. In 1497 Cabot's tiny ship sailed west with 18 men from Bristol.

Cabot hoped to find a new route to China. He landed in Newfoundland (which he thought was Asia) and set up the English flag. He saw no people but discovered the rich fishing grounds of the Grand Banks, where cod could be caught by the basketful. However, the English were disappointed to find no spices, gold or wealthy cities.

John Cabot set out again in 1498, with five ships. What happened to them is a mystery as no ships returned.

◁ **Sebastian Cabot** (about 1476-1557). He was King Henry VIII's mapmaker. He may have sailed with his father John (about 1450-1499) on the first English voyage to America. Sebastian wanted to find a 'Northeast Passage' to Asia, through Arctic waters north of Norway.

New Routes to the East

In 1500 England was no match for Spain or Portugal at sea. But by the 1550s it had a growing navy and a fleet of trading ships. Merchants paying for these ships' voyages wanted to find new trade routes to Asia, free from the influence of Spain or Portugal.

English merchants were eager to buy and sell in Asia. But the old trade route to Asia, by ship across the Mediterranean Sea and then overland through the Middle East, was beset by dangers from pirates and raiders.

▷ **Queen Elizabeth I** wanted to avoid war with Spain. But she was willing to pay for English ships to trade, take slaves and raid Spanish treasure ships.

▽ **Explorers sought a Northeast Passage**, a sea route to Asia round Scandinavia and Russia. (Left, a scene from Asia.) The Arctic seas are mostly frozen, and no Tudor ship could make such a voyage.
● Englishmen Willoughby, Chancellor and Stephen Borough, and Dutch explorer Willem Barents (about 1550-1597), all failed in their attempts to find the Northeast Passage.

There was another route from Europe to Asia – the long sea voyage round Africa and across the Indian Ocean. It was the way Portuguese sailors had reached India, the East Indies and Japan.

By the 1550s the Portuguese had warships and coastal forts along this route to stop any rivals stealing their trade. So the English looked for a new way to Asia.

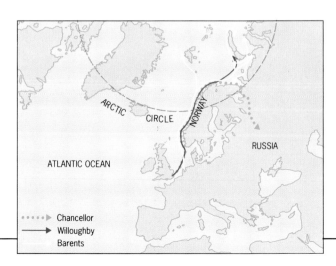

Drawing of a wealthy merchant's warehouse in about 1535. Trading voyages were risky, for a merchant's ships might be lost at sea. But a successful voyage could make him rich. Merchants formed companies to share the risks and profits of trade voyages. The Merchant Adventurers controlled English cloth sales abroad. The Muscovy (Moscow) Company was started in 1555 to trade with Russia.

Merchants sent sailors to explore the northern seas, to look for an ice-free 'passage' to Asia. In 1553 Sir Hugh Willoughby and Richard Chancellor set out with three ships to sail round Norway to "Cathay (China) and other regions, dominions, islands and places unknown". A violent storm separated Chancellor's ship from the other two, which soon became frozen in the Arctic ice. Willoughby and his companions died from cold and lack of food, but Chancellor's ship reached the north coast of Russia. He and his crew then trekked overland to Moscow, where they met the Russian emperor, Ivan IV. Ivan welcomed trade with England, and the Muscovy (Moscow) Company was set up to run it.

▷ Captain Richard Chancellor meets Ivan the Terrible, the Russian tsar (emperor). 'Terrible' meant 'awesome', though Ivan could be brutal too. The tsar welcomed the English visitors, and agreed to give English merchants trade privileges.

AN EMPIRE BEGINS

Francis Bacon, the English scientist and statesman, wrote that human beings would "extend the power and dominion of the human race over the Universe." England was not strong enough to be a power in Europe so it developed an overseas empire.

A colony in America offered new lives to people with no future in England – such as landless farmers, and Catholics and Puritans seeking religious freedom. Merchants hoped to trade with the colonies. Settlers were sent out in groups to make their homes in 'New England'.

They found no gold, but enough land for all. The Indians lived by farming, fishing and hunting. The English did the same. They learned to grow new crops, and cut timber from the forests to build their homes. The French and Spanish also had settlements in North America, but only as outposts for traders, soldiers and priests. The English were the first Europeans to settle in big numbers. Their colonists founded the British Empire, and a future nation – the United States.

▽ **A map of Virginia** by John Smith, 1624.

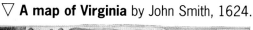

▽ **Tobacco growing** was the colonists' first trade. The English learned how to smoke from Indians, like Chief Tishcohan (below). By 1614 they were selling tobacco to England.

▽ **The settlement at Jamestown, Virginia**, was the first successful English colony in America.
● Many of the 100 or so colonists (all men) died of hunger or sickness in the first years.
● Indians were at first helpful, but then tried to fight off the newcomers.
● Women joined the colony, and families learned how to grow their own food.

GLOSSARY

Armada Spanish fleet sent to invade England in 1588.

astrolabe navigation instrument for finding latitude (a ship's position north or south of the equator).

Aztecs people of Mexico conquered by Cortés.

backstaff improved navigation instrument for finding latitude.

cannon big gun, used by ships and on land.

chart map of ocean and coasts.

colony permanent settlement founded by a country overseas.

Company group of merchants sharing in trade ventures.

convoy group of ships sailing together for protection against attack.

corn (maize or sweetcorn), a food plant unknown in Europe before the exploration of America.

courtier person attending the king or queen at court.

El Dorado mythical city of gold in America.

fleet group of ships, usually under one person's command.

galleon sailing warship, built from the mid 1500s.

Incas people of Peru conquered by Pizarro.

Indians Columbus called the people of America Indians, believing he was in the 'Indies' (Asia).

merchant trader buying and selling overseas, by sending out ships or expeditions.

musket early hand-gun.

navigation finding and maintaining a ship's correct course or direction at sea.

New World European name for North and South America.

passage route or seaway, usually to a specific location.

pike weapon like a long spear with an axe-head.

pilot navigator of a ship, often a local sailor.

plantation large farm growing one crop, such as sugarcane or bananas.

slave person held captive and forced to work.

spices plants such as pepper, cinnamon, ginger – used to flavour foods.

strait narrow channel of water, between two points of land.

tobacco plant of which dried leaves were smoked in pipes by American Indians. Pipe-smoking became popular in Europe.

TIMECHART

1492 Columbus sails to America, the first European to do so since the Vikings.

1498 John Cabot dies seeking the Northwest Passage.

1508 Sebastian Cabot explores Hudson Bay.

1513 Balboa of Spain crosses Panama and sees the Pacific Ocean.

1519-22 Magellan's round the world expedition; one ship completes the voyage.

1553 Chancellor reaches the north coast of Russia.

1560s Hawkins makes slaving voyages between Africa and America.

1578 Frobisher makes last of three voyages to North America.

1577-80 Drake sails around the world.

1580s Davis explores the North American Arctic.

1585 Raleigh pays for colonists to sail to Roanoke Island in America.

1586-88 Cavendish's voyage around the world.

1587 Colony of Roanoke in America fails.

1589 Hakluyt publishes book about the English voyages.

1595 Raleigh explores South America, looking for El Dorado.

1607 Jamestown colony in America.

1620 *Mayflower* Pilgrims sail to America.

▽ **Major regions of Tudor explorations.**

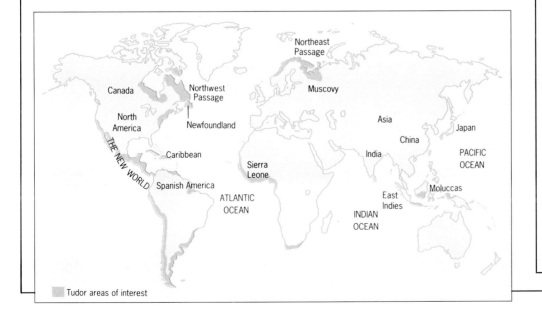

Tudor areas of interest

INDEX